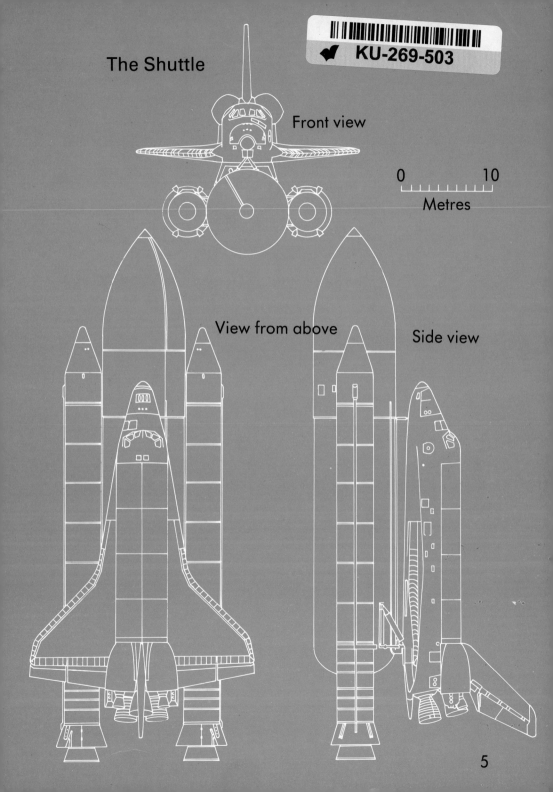

The Shuttle

Front view

Metres

View from above

Side view

0   10

Winged Rockets

German scientists in World War II (1939-45) had many plans for winged rockets. One idea, shown here, has many features in common with today's shuttle. It was to be thrust into the air by a rocket booster mounted on a single-rail track. Once in flight, the rocket's own engines would place it on course. Its flat underbody and wings would allow it to glide to targets almost halfway around the world.

Sanger-Bredt Rocket Plane

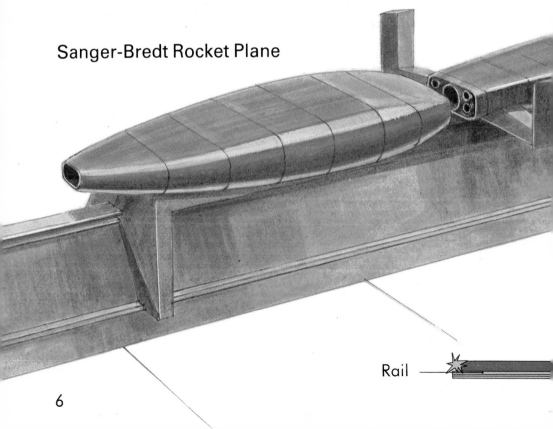

Rail

WHAT ABOUT?
SPACE SHUTTLE

Ron and Joyce Cave

Illustrated by
Roger Phillips, David West,
and Paul Cooper

FRANKLIN WATTS
London · Toronto · New York · Sydney

Space Shuttle

The space shuttle is the world's first reusable spacecraft. In the past, rockets burned up as they plunged back through Earth's atmosphere. But each shuttle can be used for as many as 50 missions. This will cut the cost of space travel considerably. The shuttle has three main parts: the shuttle spacecraft itself, an external fuel tank, and two rocket boosters. The shuttle blasts off like a rocket, moves in orbit like a spaceship, and returns home like a glider.

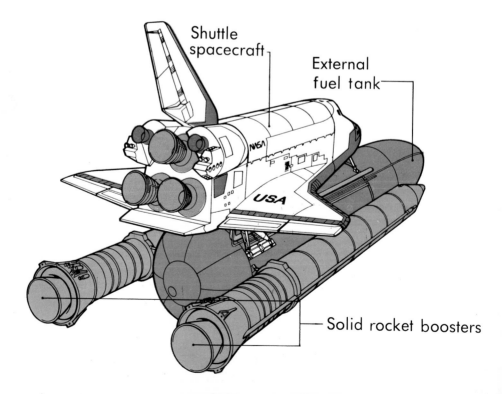

Shuttle spacecraft

External fuel tank

Solid rocket boosters

What are rocket boosters?

Rocket boosters contain almost nothing but fuel. They provide extra power to help launch a rocket or spacecraft. Once they have done their job, they are jettisoned.

Which country was first in space?

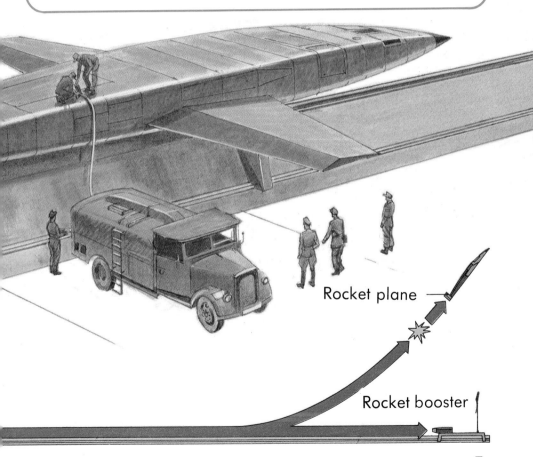

Rocket plane

Rocket booster

Early Ideas

In 1961 Yuri Gagarin, of the Soviet Union, was the first man to look back at Earth from space. Eight years later, the United States had put the first man on the Moon. During this time, many new ideas for reusable spacecraft were drawn up. Great Britain's "MUSTARD" project was to use three winged rockets of similar shape and size. These would blast off together (1), and the two outer ones would peel off at a certain height (2). These were piloted back to base (3), while the middle craft would go on into orbit (4). This craft would also be piloted home to land.

How would such spacecraft be used?

They would be used to take heavy payloads, or cargoes, into space. They could put artificial satellites into orbit, or construct space stations. Scientists could commute to these from Earth to carry out important experiments.

What are artificial satellites used for?

MUSTARD

Delta Wings

X-24B Test Craft

The shuttle does not use engines for landing. Instead, it glides through Earth's atmosphere back to base. Most gliders have large wings, but on a returning spacecraft these would become immensely hot and would burn up. Tests showed that a triangular "delta wing" design glided well and would not become too hot on re-entry. The test craft shown here was launched from under the wing of a bomber.

Why does a spacecraft become hot?

A spacecraft enters Earth's atmosphere at very high speed. At high speed, air resistance causes friction, and this creates heat. The shuttle has special heat-resistant tiles to prevent this.

Is there air resistance in space?

X-24B under the wing of a B-52 Bomber

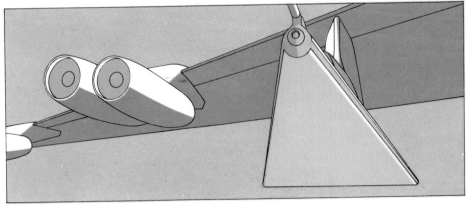

The Final Shape

A great many different ideas were considered for the final design of the shuttle. Many scientists thought that the shuttle could be launched from a piloted booster craft, as in the examples (1, 2, and 3) shown below. Others thought an ordinary space rocket could be used to get the shuttle into orbit (4). The system now used was decided upon only after many test models were made. The quarter-scale model of the complete shuttle system, shown on the right, was used to study the effects of vibration on the shuttle when it blasts off.

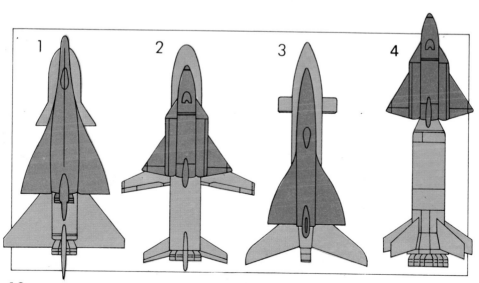

Why test for vibration?

Too much vibration could seriously damage the shuttle. The shuttle's heat-resistant tiles could shake loose, and wiring could be damaged.

Were test models flown in space?

The Enterprise

The first full-sized shuttle to be built was named the "Enterprise" after the starship in the American TV series "Star Trek." It was carried into the skies riding piggyback on a 747 jet. Enterprise's first test flight and landing was on August 12, 1977. It had no engines and will probably never fly in space.

Why didn't the Enterprise have engines?

The Enterprise was built to test the shuttle's gliding and landing ability. This must be perfect, as the crew of a returning shuttle have no engines to help them if anything goes wrong.

Are 747 jets still used to carry shuttles?

Boeing 747

Enterprise

16

Lift~off

On April 12, 1981, the three main engines of the "Columbia" roared into life. Then the booster rockets fired and the space shuttle rose majestically into the air. Two minutes after lift-off, and at a height of 43 km (27 miles), the boosters were freed to parachute into the ocean for recovery (1). At a height of 112 km (70 miles), the large fuel tank was dropped (2), to burn up as it fell to Earth. Within 11 minutes of blast-off, Columbia was in orbit 208 km (130 miles) above Earth (3).

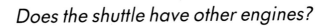

Does the shuttle have other engines?

The shuttle's three main engines are used only in lift-off. Two smaller engines are used to position the shuttle in space. They also slow the craft down before the shuttle begins its homeward journey. Small rocket thruster engines allow the shuttle to be piloted very accurately when it is in orbit.

Who was on board Columbia?

3

Shuttle in Space

By the end of the 1980s a fleet of shuttles may have made several hundred space flights. Apart from launching satellites, some flights will be to build space stations. Also, large companies are interested in carrying out experiments in space. So, certain shuttles, like the one illustrated, will carry a specially-built space laboratory, called the "Spacelab," into orbit around Earth.

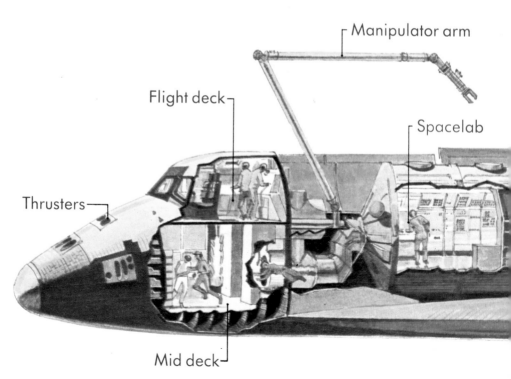

Manipulator arm

Flight deck

Spacelab

Thrusters

Mid deck

What is the Spacelab exactly?

The Spacelab fits into the shuttle's cargo bay. Inside, scientists will be able to carry out experiments outside the pull of Earth's gravity. Spacelab stays on the shuttle throughout its flight.

What experiments will scientists do?

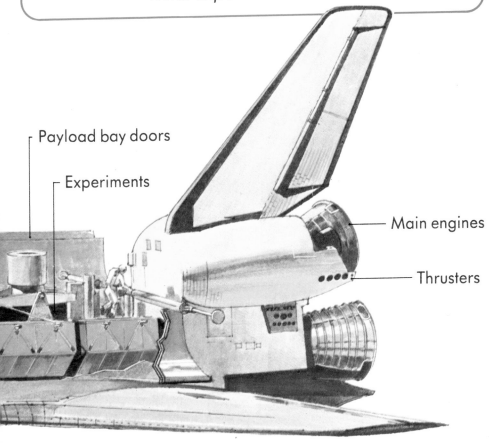

Payload bay doors

Experiments

Main engines

Thrusters

Inside the Cabin

The shuttle has a flight crew of two: the commander and co-pilot. Two extra crew members can also be carried to do experiments in the Spacelab or to take care of the shuttle's cargo. While in orbit, the crew can work in their shirtsleeves, without bulky space suits. Slipper-like footholds on the floor help to stop the crew from floating about in the weightlessness of space.

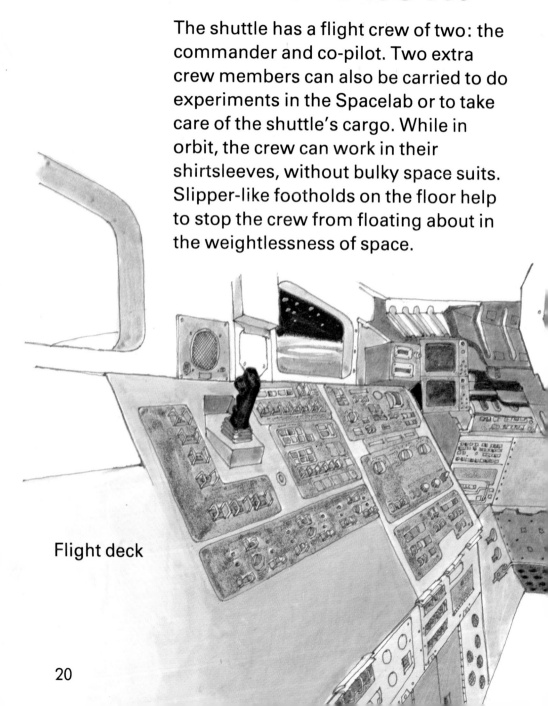

Flight deck

Are the crew all trained astronauts?

The commander and co-pilot will always be astronauts with at least three years' training. But scientists carried on board require only two months' basic training before their flight. There is an age limit of fifty years on all crew.

Could tourists fly in the shuttle?

Shuttlenauts

Shuttlenaut is simply the name given to people flying in the shuttle. The shuttlenauts will only need to wear space suits when they leave the shuttle, perhaps to repair a satellite, or build a space station. Each space suit will be fitted with two-way radios and a small computer. Each shuttlenaut will move in space by using the small gas thruster jets on his backpack.

How long can the shuttle stay up?

The first test orbit of the Columbia lasted for just over two days. Future flights can be extended for as long as a month. But the shuttle was designed to carry cargo and supply space stations rather than for long stays in orbit.

What kind of food do the shuttlenauts eat?

Return to Earth

On its return to Earth, the shuttle changes from a spacecraft into a giant glider. First, its rockets fire for the last time to position the craft and slow it down. As it glides down, its speed drops from over 28,000 kph (17,000 mph) to about 350 kph (218 mph) at touchdown. Although the shuttle can be flown manually, landing is normally done under computer control.

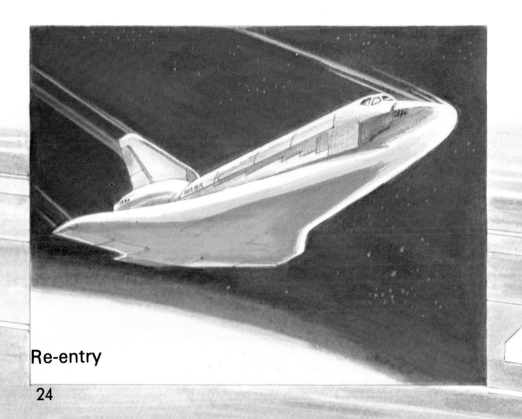

Re-entry

How soon after landing is the shuttle ready for relaunch?

Within an hour of touchdown the shuttle is towed to a workshop. Then it is checked down to the last nut and bolt. In two weeks the shuttle can be ready for another lift-off.

How big is the shuttle?

Chase plane

Landing

The Future

The space age has hardly begun, but giant steps forward have already been made. Future plans are for manned space stations and giant solar power stations, like the one being built in the picture. There may even be space factories. These projects will cost huge sums of money, but the shuttle has brought them within our reach. The future looks very exciting.

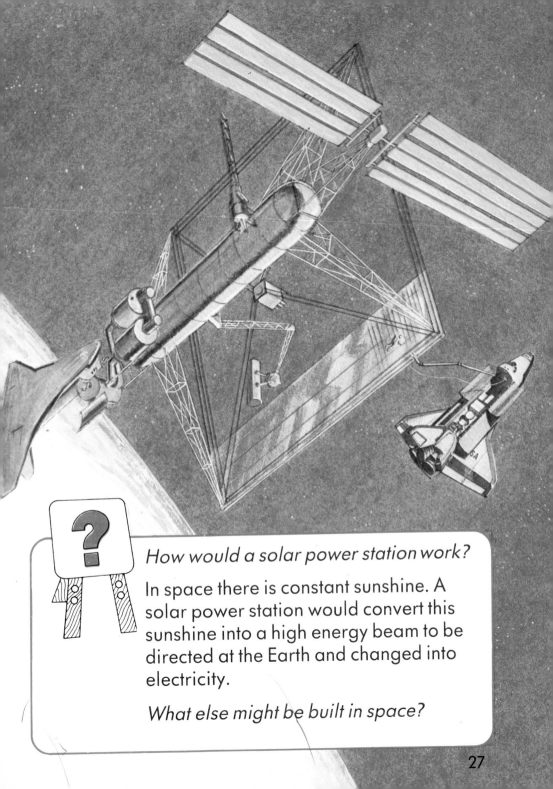

How would a solar power station work?

In space there is constant sunshine. A solar power station would convert this sunshine into a high energy beam to be directed at the Earth and changed into electricity.

What else might be built in space?

Answers

Which country was first in space?

The Soviet Union in 1957, with Sputnik I.

What are artificial satellites used for?

They have many uses. Some send television pictures around the world. Satellites are used to study the Earth, or predict the weather. Others are used to spy on enemy countries.

Is there air resistance in space?

There is no air in space to give resistance. Going into orbit means escaping Earth's atmosphere entirely.

Were test models flown in space?

No. The first shuttle to fly in space was the Columbia, a full-sized working shuttle.

Are 747 jets still used to carry shuttles?

Yes. Shuttles have no engines to fly on their own, so 747 jets are used to ferry them to their launch sites.

Who was on board Columbia?

The flight commander was John Young, and Robert Crippen was his co-pilot.

What experiments will scientists do?

There is no gravity, or pulling force, in space. This means that space is the ideal place to make very pure products such as medicines, or sensitive electronic equipment. Certain metals refuse to mix on Earth, will they in space? These are the sort of experiments which will be carried out.

Could tourists fly in the shuttle?

Pleasure trips into space may be a possibility in the future. The shuttle's cargo bay could be fitted out to carry passengers.

What kind of food do the shuttlenauts eat?

Three-course hot meals, similar to the food served on passenger jets, will be prepared on the shuttle.

How big is the shuttle?

It is about the size of a medium-size jetliner. It is 37 m (122 ft) long and has a wingspan of 24 m (78 ft).

Index